Matthias Wörne

Treasures in the Sunshine

Poems

Matthias Wörne

Treasures in the Sunshine

Poems

Bibliografische Information der Deutschen Nationalbibliothek:
Die Deutsche Nationalbibliothek verzeichnet diese Publikation in der
Deutschen Nationalbibliografie; detaillierte bibliografische Daten sind
im Internet über http://dnb.dnb.de abrufbar.

Cover Design: Muriel Wörne

Herstellung und Verlag: BoD – Books on Demand, Norderstedt

ISBN: 9783755727149

"While they were eating Tom went up to the mound, and looked through the treasures. Most of these he made into a pile that glistened and sparkled on the grass. He bade them lie there 'free to all finders, birds, beast, Elves or Men, and all kindly creatures'; for so the spell of the mound should be broken and scattered and no Wight ever come back to it."

J.R.R. Tolkien: The Fellowship of the Ring

In your Head

In your head
a thousand
voices ...
thoughts ...
ideas ...

shhhhhhh ...
         hush ...
            listen ...

to the world ...
to life ...
here ...
now ...

Early in the Morning

it was just a car that passed outside
early in the morning
as we still lay in bed
but I listened to it
as if it were a long deep breath you took
and I felt the breathing in my own body
and it brought to me a faint hint
a suggestion of something I can almost but do not
    remember
something that is lost forever
in ages past

Ideas and Swallows

so many ideas and swallows
all alone or
in clusters forming and dissolving
chirping
fluttering
gliding along
doing unexpected turns
in the overcast morning sky

how beautiful just to watch them
in their wild ways
trusting the air
trusting their wings
trusting the world
enjoying the freedom of
space

Birdsong (Haiku)

Birdsong. Intense blue.
Flowers sprawl across empty
diary pages.

written in March 2020 during lockdown

Waters of the Soul

Mighty are the waters of the soul

      wave after wave after wave
      moving and formed by a force

never, in no way under control

The Flower and the Seed

The flower is here for the sake of the seed.
And the seed is here for the sake of the flower.

If the flower does not wilt and harden,
life is not renewed.

If the seed does not get buried,
does not soften, open, crack,
life is not renewed.

And the flower is here
for its own sake,
for the flowering,
for the expression
of fragrance, colour, beauty.

And the seed is here
for being the seed:
essence, concentration
of what is.

And in being what they are,
Life
Is.

Enveloped

notice and feel
how the earth envelops herself
how you are enveloped too
in a cloak of cooling clouds
a fine mist
a soothing poultice
the moisture a relief
for the drought
the wounds of the past

healing is happening
and you are nurtured
and you may
let it happen
let it be
and feel the pulse of life
in your heart
in your body
and all around

Embedded

listening
to the world

listening
to my breathing

connecting my breathing
with the breathing
of the land
my breathing embedded
a part of the breathing of
life
here

the daily breathing of night and day
the breathing of weather
the whirling and moving of air in the aura of Earth
wind from the West and Southwest
from the North or the East
the breathing of seasons
distinct but slow
and the long long breathing in and breathing out
of ages cold and ages warm

and below
the pulse
of the moving of Earth
uplifting eroding
colliding and drifting apart
the erupting of hidden fire
into the visible
the cooling of the molten

feeling my pulse
calm and steady
as a rhythm
a pulsing
among others
some slower
some quicker
the pulsing of life
here
in this land

Nightingale

Vigorous.
Passionate.
Creative.
And so intense.

Hidden in the undergrowth
you sound your voice
through hours
in the very middle of the night.

Using every tiny muscle in your throat,
making sounds unheard of,
testing, probing,
and yet so sure.

Giving it your all
as if your very life depended on it,
as if nothing else mattered.

How can such a small being
make such an array of incredible noises?
How and where
do you find these sounds?
Who whispers them to you?

Mesmerized
I lie still.
Listen.
And nothing else matters.

Pont-de-Vaux, May 2015

Fragile

Danger everywhere!
Hawks, cats, parasites!
Storm and nasty weather!

Will your feathers keep you warm?
Will you always find a safe place to hide?
Will you be cautious enough
not to be taken by surprise?

Will you travel great distances?
Will you come back one day?
Will you build your own nest?

May I trust in your strength
in your wit
your resilience?

Oh, what an adventure life is!
How fragile –
no guarantees whatsoever.

Cueva de Orandi

all this rushing water
disappearing in an opening
between the rocks
a cleft I cannot enter
falling straight into
the underworld

close by
on the meadow
a horse is quietly grazing
eyeing me from time to time

and a little further down
right below the sacred cave
water pours out of a rock wall
into a pool
made to receive it

Covadonga/Asturias, October 2019

Water

„Quelle des größten Stroms in Mitteleuropa"
„Mutter Baar, Tochter Donau"
„Andauernder Kampf zwischen Donau und Rhein"

all this big talk
all this drama
is just
water
following its way

Donaueschingen, July 2020

Laki

What a strange beauty ...
this desolate devastated landscape.
The power of
      what is it: heat, pressure,
      wrath, subterranean energy?
has created a world of its own.
All that was before
the lush meadows
are buried
covered
with molten and petrified rock.

Look at these forms.
Follow the lines, the contours
of mountains and valleys
with your eyes.

Look at the colours
the countless hues
the nuances of green
the rocks dark black grey
the spots of reddish brown.

Look at how lichen and moss
cover the lava's sharp edges.

Look.
Take it in.

And remember how you have seen
– in other but similar places –
trees and flowers eventually take root.

And remember
that in such a landscape
there is potential enough
for a good and fertile life.

I tell you:
I myself I grew up in a place like that.

Iceland (qualities and attractions)

the colours
the light
the gloom
the brightness
green
earth power
the wind the wind
the sparseness bleakness
the strangeness
the rejectiveness
the beauty
the birdiness

Followed the call of love

followed the call of love
yes listened to its voice
stayed true to it – at last
became its fool

now standing here
in fog
slowed down
not even in the distance
a horizon to be seen
nothing to give advice
of way, direction – no just

      void

         void

            void all around
            void all inside

what shall I do
where shall I go
in which direction shall I turn
my face?

oh that a star would fall
out of the sky and land
beside me – I would gladly
pick it up and treasure it
and carry it
to you

My Longing

My soul to be
seen
appreciated

My self to be
loved
as I am

Me encouraged
on my way,
bringing my gifts
into the world.

The Hero the Fool

Look at the poor guy coming!
Look at the hero the fool!
Greet him
and invite him in!
He braved wind, rain, cold, hunger, thirst.
He braved his demons.
He has arrived.
Give him bread and give him wine.
Pour a bath for him.
Put fresh clothes before him
and anoint his feet.
Let him rest.
He is here,
he has made it.
Welcome him!

Turn turn turn

To every thing
turn turn turn
there is a season
turn turn turn   (Pete Seeger)

There is a time
to cling to what you love
with all the strength in your
arms
hands
fingernails
heart
and mind

to hold on to it
to let it drag you
through thick undergrowth
over sharp stones
that rip your skin open
to let it bruise you
through and through
until your whole body hurts
and you don't know any more
who you are
where you are
and where you are headed

and there is a time
to let go
to open your fingers
and let the thing
or the person
you hold so dear
– as dear as your soul –
fly into the air
back into the hands of
Life itself
not knowing
what will become
of it
– or her or him –
of you

accepting forces greater than yours
without the slightest understanding
of why
and if ever

laying yourself into these hands
and trying to trust
that you are well kept there

and allowing your wounds to heal

Words

„Spoken words are like runaway dogs" (from Kenya)

What I have built I can tear down
Put down what I have put up
Loosen what I have fixed

I can
uncover
unfold
unhook
unload
unravel
unseal
unwind
unwrap

but how

can I unsay what I have said?
Unwrite what I have written?
Unsend what I have sent?

The only thing to say is "sorry " ...
                      ... and be silent

Will you unhear what you have heard?
Will you unreject me?
Will you forgive me? Pardon me?
Will you listen anew?

Realizing
Grace

Lost

Being lost
at a loss
not knowing
why
what
where
who
when

just
not
knowing

accepting this state of mind
this state of being

breathing

doing what has to be done
not doing what cannot be done

being
waiting

breathing

Undercover

under the guise
under the cover
of attraction
longing
even need
there might lie
a well
of unconditional love
healing power
priceless gift
freely given
where you might or you might not
scoop and drink
in sips and mouthfuls
or even bathe or swim
as long as you ever want

So intense

this yearning
for spring
and a warm
wind
breath
word
to melt these ice-encrusted hidden places
in my soul

Oh Love ...

hurtful,
difficult,
inconvenient,
bringing conflict,
bringing sorrow ...

But what a gift of life you are!
How you open my heart
to the world!

Dreams of Hope

No more rabbits on Macquarie
No more mice on the Antipodes
Devils thriving on Maria
Mohua, Tieke and Kakariki singing their songs on Ulva
Kakapo booming on Codfish
Islands of Hope

No more pesticides in nature reserves
No more logging in old-growth forest
No more mining in the Amazon

A stop of the fighting in the Donbass
A sabbatical of the armaments industry
Taliban discovering tolerance
Israelites and Palestinians laughing together beside
       a spring they share
Bumblebees and butterflies fluttering in my garden
Wild pockets of land spreading from Mount Beauty
       to the plains

Me staying true to who I am
You softening your heart just a little
Us giving up the attachment to our wounds

No more violence in my speech
An impossibility becoming real
Your call

The Spell Broken

The spell broken.
The trip over.
The hero returned.
The knot loosened.
Found what was lost.

Clouds breaking up.
The lump dissolving.
The hurt healing.
Heaviness rooted.

Two Red Kites
soaring over the Hill
calling
circling
gracefully
without effort
and light
as a feather.

A Ring

is a reminder
is a token
is not a guarantee
is a connection
a bond
is not part of a chain
and yet a link
between two separate beings
each infinite and
whole on its own

Feathers

for Anja

May our love be as light as a feather
May our love be as soft as a feather
May our love be as strong as a feather

May our love
enfold and warm us
protect us
carry us
be our beauty
like a bird's feathers

May our love be renewed
again and again
like the feathers of a bird

Totara Tree

Over seasons and seasons and seasons
over years and years and years
our love has grown

we've seen storms and fires
felt hail and quaking earth
some branches have been broken off
but the trunk is a pillar
and our roots have grown and grown

and after a thousand years or more
our love is still alive
and stronger than ever

A Work of Art

Your life: a work of art.
A story you write.
A picture you paint.
A song you compose.

Enjoy the creating.
Let it surprise you.
Do it carefully:
each word,
each chord,
each brushstroke.
May it bring colour,
sound,
beauty and
joy
to the world

New Zealand Poems

The following poems were written between 2016 and 2019 during and after traveling on the South Island of New Zealand.

Avon River

A slowly winding river flows
through the grid-patterned city.
In its quiet waters willows bathe their leaves
as it travels leisurely
the last remaining miles
to the wild Pacific Sea.

Christchurch

Lake Matheson

Late in the afternoon
all our noisy walking and talking
and scenery-click-clicking
drops
into the depth of your
dark quiet waters
is absorbed by the timeless
forest on your shores
and turns again into
silence

Underwater
the long-finned eel is getting ready
for his hunt
of unwary prey

Lake Matheson, West Coast

Morning in Fox Glacier (Haiku)

Helicopter blades
chopping beauty and silence
into bits and pieces

Fox Glacier, World Heritage Area

Far far away (Haiku)

Far far away a
radiant boat on the sea
is floating – and gone.

Sunset at Cape Foulwind, West Coast

Moa

Your enormous legs still walk through our dreams.
Your eyes look down at us, astonished,
unbelieving.

Hokioi

Giant Eagle, where are you?
The sky looks empty without you circling high above.
And though the rush of your wings meant wonder and
       terror at the same time,
I miss the sound of them
and your call.

But you have flown to the land beyond –
and we had our share in this.
Gone you are
and yet I wonder:
Is your spirit lingering?
Are you watching the mountains and the forest from
       somewhere up high
this land that was yours for ages?
Could you even be a guardian
protecting the land
determined and of great strength?

I wish you back –
and the other ones, too
who are also gone.
Your kin.

Is your power lost forever to the world
lost to us?
Or could we at least
– by talk, by songs, by stories, by dance –
honor you
keep you in memory and so
bring back some of your gifts to this world we live in?

The Haast's Eagle was a species of eagle that once lived in New Zealand. The species was the largest eagle known to have existed. Haast's Eagle became extinct around 1400, after the moa were hunted to extinction by the first Māori. There are Māori stories that tell about "Hokioi", a bird which may have been the Eagle and which was able even to kill humans.

The Eros of Falling Water

intense longing to be reunited
falling like rivers of tears from the mountains
tears of yearning
tears of joy
ecstasy of roaring
rushing
gushing
spreading across the valleys
covering all and not minding it
no waiting
no lingering

straight home

and then
the next day:

peace
quiet
beauty
fulfilment
sun shining on the tranquil waters of the fiord

and yet
look closer:

a layer of fresh water lying
above the salty sea
not mixing
not mingling
staying apart
creating a unique habitat
of light and dark

Milford Track & Milford Sound

Big Totara

Ancient One
Elder
standing like a monument
but alive
a living being many times as old as I

How many generations of grey warblers have sung
        in your branches
you who were already old in the age of the moa
who saw and heard voices we will never again listen to
whose songs are forever gone?

Nothing there that can surprise you anymore.
No storm you fear
no quake of the earth.
Though even you don't live forever
such happenings do not concern you much.

Silently you stand among your kin
– elders like you and many young ones –
listening rather than talking much
as wise as any of your tribe becomes.

Our words and notions mean nothing to you
and we are not your concern.

But nonetheless
your mere existence and appearance
have a profound effect on anyone
who stays a while in your presence
and is restored
to the deeper and larger scheme of things

Peel Forest

To Be a Tree

Oh to be a tree!

Being just myself
standing here without any questions
this being a good place for me to stand
living my life as
kahikatea
rimu
rata
beech
standing
growing
breathing
living my life
and at the same time
being and meaning so much more
to other beings
an anchor
or even a home
or a birthplace
for thousands
– yes indeed thousands –
of other beings
mosses
ferns
lichens
clinging to my trunk and to my branches
not needing more than this
insects in my bark
under my skin

birds using the shelter of holes and leaves
hunting for insects
building nests
tending their young
or just resting a while

Oh to be a tree!

Haast Beach

Lessons from a Kiwi

Meet me, yes.
I am here around.
But meet me on my terms.

Stay quiet.
Keep some distance.
And I don't like strong light.

I am a creature of dusk and dark
so meet me in the twilight
and be content
that you don't see me
as distinctly as you would like.

Anyway:
it is an encounter
a meeting in two ways.

I am very different from you.
My life
my habits
are not like yours.
Still we can meet
and in some way
we are siblings
though distant.

But don't blend me with your bright light.
Be quiet and
keep some distance
please.

And note:
Forgiving is possible – even between us.
Last night you turned your bright torchlight on me.
Accidentally.
I stayed.
I waited.
And you did not do it again.

Port William Hut, Stewart Island

Identity

Canoes from Hawaiki
origins
ancestors
journeys across the endless ocean
remembering
acknowledging
honoring
your past
your heritage

How long does it take
until the roots you have grown in this land of forests and
        mountains and birds
are so deep
the bonds so strong
and your being here so woven in
intertwined
entangled
that you feel that above all
you belong to this place as a native
that you have risen from this soil
from these rocks
in these valleys
that you have been born from this land
that you are at home right here?

It may take a thousand years.
It may have just begun.
It may be continued.

Changing mythology.
Changing identity.

And the stars that turn above your heads
who guided your forebears to these shores
will continue to remind you
of other stories
not to be forgotten.

Bubbling

Bubbling and bubbling
Incessantly bubbling
Bubbling and healing
Endlessly healing
Clear water bubbling
Showing the beauty
beneath the surface
Peacefully flowing
Restoring my life

Te Waikoropupu Springs

This is in honor of those who stayed

This is in honor of those who stayed: those who did not leave their place, who saw the destruction and the ruins of what they had built, who felt the loss and heartbreak – and stayed. Those who took to work and to shovels and excavators and who gracefully accepted the help and support they got from one another and from people they didn't even know.

This is in honor of those who accepted that their work would take a long long time and over a generation of lives and that there was and is no guarantee at all that this place was or is any safer now than before, that it will ever be really safe – but who nonetheless believed that beauty and a life well worth living could be created anew in this very place and who found the courage and the vision of this re-creating inside their hearts.

This is in honor of those who do the slow and steady work of re-building and of building anew and whose work is an inspiration for many others and a sign of hope and strength and healing in an unstable and sometimes broken world.

Christchurch

RE:Start

Knowing it may always happen again
shaking the foundations of your world
destroying what you have built
opening gaps that can swallow you
because of hidden forces you
don't see
can't see
have no idea of
cannot understand nor foresee the dynamics of
and don't have the slightest chance
to influence or change...

Being thankful
for all the quiet and peaceful days
with sunshine and rain
doing what you can do
to adjust yourself to this place
to create beauty and stability
as far as it is possible

And after much has been destroyed
– no, not everything! –
and you live and will live
among the ruins and wounds for a long while:

Starting to rebuild what is broken
to mend the holes and wounds
tearing things completely down
steadying others that are shaken but still standing

and then
eventually
even rebuilding what was
and might be again
the most beautiful heart of the place

Christchurch

Disaster

Again
disaster has hit you
a shock of a different kind
human
– or rather: man-made –
unforeseen
completely knocking you
and us all
off your feet and balance

and you
cry
mourn
show your solidarity
with those hit by hate and madness

and you
stand together as one
express
love
peace
tolerance
instead of hate and vengeance.

and you do
what has to be done
and one more time
we are
impressed
moved
affected
inspired
strengthened and
encouraged
to follow your example
and make this world a better place

Ebringen, March 2019,
after the terrorist attacks on two mosques in Christchurch

Beautiful Journey

A journey in search of beauty
became a journey of beauty
a beauty-full journey

I will weave a silken cocoon around it
place it in a polished wooden box
protect it from scratches and stains
and let its beauty continue to shine

Ebringen, 2019

Curio Bay Longing

to get up early and
walk over to the big window looking east
see the light and the colours slowly change behind
       the headland jutting out into the Pacific Sea
watch another sunrise
feel the wind coming up and moving the flax behind
       the lawn

get a glimpse of somebody walking along the beach
looking forward to a day in one of the most beautiful
       places on earth
looking out for the dolphins
and maybe this time
joining them in the water
for a little while

Ebringen, December 2020

Lord of the Rings Poems

The poems that follow were inspired by the reading of "The Fellowship of the Ring", the first volume of "The Lord of the Rings" by J.R.R. Tolkien. They were written in January 2021

Mirrormere

dark and clear
deep and calm
a mirror to the star-filled world
no shadow of your silhouette

Silverlode

crystal clear
icy cold
a springing from beneath the rocks
a silver thread to follow

Silverlode and Mirrormere

a lake of dark blue waters
with still unruffled face
a lake with an unbroken rim
that draws you, hurt and weary

clear and deep like the evening sky
seen from a lamp-lit room
and as you stand and look into
its depth, no shadow of your self

is to be seen – instead
the snow-capped mountains gleam
and though it is still daylight
the stars like jewels glint

and not far from the Mirrormere
there springs the Silverlode
its waters crystal clear and cold
its course for you to follow

In the Barrow

In the barrow
the cold is as chilling
as a winter night

In the barrow
the grip clutching you is as strong
as an iron chain

In the barrow
you are frozen to your bones and marrow
unable to move limb or even eyelid

Lying in the barrow
dread is all around and inside you
the spell of a nameless energy
holds you imprisoned

The barrow
is a curse
is a tomb
is a railing of a power against that
of what it is bereaved
for what it yearns
and hungers

and it wishes you stone-dead

As you are lying in the barrow
there is inside you
a strand of memory
of sunshine
stars
stories
merry voices
and laughter

As you are lying in the barrow
hidden deep inside you is
a seed of
courage
an unexpected strength
a resolve and a stiffening
as for a final spring

In the dark of the barrow
you are no longer helpless
paralyzed
but willing to fight

In your mind
there is the remembered sounding
of a song
and from your heart to your throat
there rises your voice
thin and tentative at first
but growing stronger by itself
until it echoes and booms
throughout the whole chamber

And through the walls of the barrow
you hear an answering voice
an answering song
that is stronger than the incantations of the curse
stronger than the walls of the tomb

and you hear a loud rumbling and
suddenly
a flood of light streams in
the light of the day
and your heart and limbs begin to warm

The Song of Bombadil

As you are lying in the dark
afraid, imprisoned, bleak and chilled
there is a corner in your mind
remembering Tom Bombadil.

And as you think of his old hat
there comes to you like sudden gift
the rhyme he taught you, learned by heart:
the melody of Bombadil.

And so you start to sing the tune,
your voice is booming in the tomb
and through the ground and the thick walls
you hear the voice of Bombadil.

In rumbling loud stones roll and fall
then light so bright and warm you feel,
a door appears – and suddenly
there is again Tom Bombadil!

He is all merry and all song,
all dread is banished, disappears.
You shout for joy and know that you never again
forget the song of Bombadil.

Lay the Treasures in the Sunshine

Lay the treasures of the barrow
in the sunshine, in the grass!
They are not meant to stay hidden,
rust or crumble underground.

They are free for all who find them,
to be taken with kind heart.
Thus the barrow's spell is broken,
banished is the dread, the cold.
Joy and strength and hope will flow.

The Gift

star-glass
precious gift
shining brightness
pure light
morning token
caught and contained
in fountain water
freshly sprung
to be carried
on your breast

a light to you in darkest places
when other lights have all gone out
for giving strength against all menace
for hope to grow strong in your mind

Contents

New Zealand Poems

Lord of the Rings Poems

You can find more information
about the author on
www.matthiaswoerne.de